C000104335

Why Go to Mass?

by
Michael Evans

*All booklets are published thanks to the
generous support of the members of the
Catholic Truth Society*

CATHOLIC TRUTH SOCIETY
PUBLISHERS TO THE HOLY SEE

Contents

Introduction...3

Catechism of Catholic Church............................4

Celebrating the Christian Mystery.....................5

The Eucharist and the Mystery of the Trinity.............7

Thanksgiving to the Father..................................7

Sacrificial Memorial of Christ.............................8

An Easter Communion.......................................11

The Church's living memory...............................13

New meaning, new Value...................................14

The presence of Christ.......................................15

Through faith not the senses.............................17

Historical thought...18

Reception and Adoration...................................20

Christ the Priest..21

The Mass of all Ages..22

Communion with Christ.....................................23

Communion with one another............................25

Communion with the poor and oppressed.........27

'Ite, missa est'..28

A service to others..29

Forward to the Future.......................................30

Sacrament of Love..31

INTRODUCTION

'Going to Mass' has always been a key sign of a committed Catholic, from those first Christians who met in their houses for 'the breaking of bread' (Acts 2:42, 46), to Catholics who risked their lives by celebrating Mass during times of persecution, to those Catholics today who make a conscious choice to take an active part in the life and worship of the Church. In every century there have been Catholics who have opted out of the Church's worship, but taking part in the Mass, above all on Sundays, has always been seen as central and crucial for living fully the Catholic faith and life. Coming to Mass, taking part in a Catholic Eucharist every Sunday, is still the main visible sign of being a Catholic. Living the Mass, taking an active part in it and allowing its power to transform our lives, is what being a Catholic is all about (see the *Catechism of the Catholic Church*, nn. 1389, 2177–9; all references are to this Catechism unless otherwise noted).

The central importance of the Mass or Eucharist is something strongly reaffirmed by the *Catechism*: the Eucharist is 'the source and summit of ecclesial life', 'the sum and summary of our faith' (n. 1327), 'the most blessed Sacrament' and 'the Sacrament of sacraments' (nn. 1211, 1330), and it 'remains the centre of the

Church's life' (n. 1343). Why? Because it 'contains' and makes present the living mystery of Christ, Christ himself and his saving work of bringing the whole human race into communion with his Father. If we really understood the Good News of Jesus Christ, the Good News of salvation, and if we grasped fully the truth that the Eucharist is the making present here and now of all that Jesus has achieved for us, we would need no urging to come to Mass.

The Catechism of the Catholic Church

The *Catechism* gives us the essential content of the Catholic faith in the light of the Second Vatican Council and of the whole of the Church's Tradition. Obviously, therefore, there is nothing radically different about its teaching on the Eucharist, but there are refreshingly new ways of looking at the ancient doctrine.

The very first article of the *Catechism* reminds us of God's overall plan: God draws close to us so that we can share his own life; he calls us to seek him, know him and love him; he calls us together into the unity of his family, the Church. This is the key to understanding the mystery of the Eucharist.

As Christ's Eucharistic people, we are all challenged to develop our doctrine on the Eucharist, to mature in our Eucharistic faith, and to become ever more deeply Eucharistic persons and communities (n. 23).

Celebrating the Christian Mystery

Many think that Part Two of the *Catechism* (Celebrating the Christian Mystery) is its best. In presenting the liturgy and sacraments, it is especially open to the insights of Eastern Christians, particularly in its emphasis on the role of the Holy Spirit. The order of the *Catechism* is significant: Creed (our faith professed), Sacraments (our faith celebrated), Commandments (our faith lived), rather than Creed, Commandments, Sacraments. The latter order can lead to understanding the sacraments simply as powerful aids to keeping the Commandments, rather than as the key ways in which we share in the mystery of Christ here and now, a participation which leads us to a new way of life.

We come to Mass to share in the wonder of our Father's love, to participate in the saving work of Jesus his Son, and to be transformed by the Spirit of holiness. From our Sunday celebration, we go forth together to be and to live what we have celebrated. For the rest of the week (or for the rest of the day if we go to Mass more often) our life as Christian communities, families and individuals flows from the Mass and looks towards the next celebration. Every Mass is also a reminder that there is a greater life to come: in the Eucharist we already share that heavenly life, and look forward to its fulfilment: 'We hope to enjoy for ever the vision of your glory' (Eucharistic Prayer 3).

All of this may seem strange to any Catholics who come to Mass simply because they have always done so, because they see it merely as their 'Sunday obligation', or because someone else – parents perhaps, or school - demands they come. Why does the Catholic Church insist so strongly on the need to come to Mass? We all need to think more deeply about the Mass and what it means. In this short pamphlet I can do no more than give a few thoughts for reflection, rooted in the *Catechism*. There is so much more that can be said.

THE EUCHARIST AND THE MYSTERY OF THE TRINITY

One special merit of the *Catechism* is its emphasis on the Holy Trinity as the central mystery of our faith. This is especially true of its teaching on the liturgy, the Church's public worship. The Father is the source and goal of the liturgy. In and through the risen Christ, the Paschal Mystery is continued in the sacraments: 'Christ is always present to his Church, especially in her liturgical celebrations' (n. 1088). The Holy Spirit is 'the artisan of God's masterpieces, the sacraments of the new covenant' (n. 1091). God's own beauty and artistry are expressed in a special way in the Church's liturgy.

The *Catechism* discusses the Eucharist under three main Trinitarian headings: as thanksgiving and praise to the Father; as the sacrificial memorial of Christ and of his Body, the Church; as the presence of Christ by the power of his Word and of the Holy Spirit (n. 1358).

Thanksgiving to the Father

'Eucharist' means first of all 'thanksgiving' (n. 1360). It is a sacrifice of thanksgiving to the Father, a sacrament of gratitude in which the Church sings glory to God in the name of all creation (n. 1361).

In the Eucharistic sacrifice the whole of creation loved by God is presented to the Father through the death and resurrection of Christ. Through Christ the Church can offer the sacrifice of praise in thanksgiving for all that God has made good, beautiful and just in creation and in humanity (n. 1359).

Is this dimension of thanksgiving central enough to our own understanding and celebration of the Eucharist? Do we come to the Eucharist consciously united with all creation in praise of the Father, simply to lift up our hearts to God because 'it is right to give him thanks and praise'?

Sacrificial Memorial of Christ

The *Catechism* echoes the central importance of the concept of 'memorial' for biblical, patristic (Church Fathers) and modern Eucharistic theology. A 'memorial' involves far more than simply remembering what happened once-upon-a-time:

In the sense of Sacred Scripture the memorial is not merely the recollection of past events but the proclamation of the mighty works wrought by God for men. In the liturgical celebration of these events, they become in a certain way present and real. This is how Israel understands its liberation from Egypt: every

time Passover is celebrated the Exodus events are
made present to the memory of believers so that they
may conform their lives to them (n. 1363).

The Passover is a ritual meal, celebrated as a
'memorial' of the great escape from slavery in Egypt
and the entry of God's people into a new friendship, a
new covenant with God. The Jewish idea of memorial
involves evoking the past in such a way that a past
event is made effective and fruitful here and now.
The heart of the event itself is made present for us
today (n. 1334).

Jesus took the Passover Meal and fulfilled its
deepest meaning. He transformed it into the memorial
of his own saving death and resurrection. The heart of
Jesus' saving work is made present for us here and
now: in the Eucharist, Jesus himself is personally
present as our crucified and risen Saviour (n. 1340).
There we powerfully 'proclaim the death of the Lord
until he comes' (1 Cor 11:26). It is Jesus himself who
tells us to 'Do this as a memorial of me' (1 Cor 11:24,
25), and when we come to Mass we keep his special
commandment of love.

A 'sacrificial' understanding of the Eucharist is the
heart of Catholic teaching on the Mass. This is clearly
reaffirmed in the *Catechism* in a way which makes full
use of the New Testament language of memorial:

The Eucharist is the memorial of Christ's Passover, the making present and the sacramental offering of his unique sacrifice, in the liturgy of the Church which is his Body (n. 1362).

When the Church celebrates the Eucharist, she commemorates Christ's Passover, and it is made present: the sacrifice Christ offered once for all on the cross remains ever present (n. 1364).

'Memorial' is a biblical way of presenting our later idea of 'sacrament'. The liturgical celebration of the Eucharist is the outward, visible sign of the inward, invisible grace of Christ's gift of salvation. The Eucharist is the 'sacrament of salvation'. We call it a sacrifice because 'it re-presents (makes present) the sacrifice of the cross, because it is its memorial and because it applies its fruit' (n. 1366). This means that 'the sacrifice of Christ and the sacrifice of the Eucharist are one single sacrifice' (n. 1367). By taking part in the Eucharist, we participate in Christ's saving sacrifice, his death and resurrection.

This means that the Eucharist is much more than a Communion Service at which the Scriptures are read and Holy Communion is given. In some Catholic churches, a deacon or lay minister leads such a service when there is no priest to preside at a celebration of the Eucharist. Such services are of great value when a priest cannot be present, but they are not the Mass and are ultimately no substitute for the Mass itself.

An Easter Communion

The Eucharist is the memorial of the death and resurrection of Christ (nn. 1323, 1330, 1337, 1341). This is an advance on some previous theology which understood the Eucharist as the memorial or sacramental representation only of the death or cross of Christ, rather than of the total mystery of salvation. Each Eucharist is therefore an Eastertidal moment, and there should be a note of 'festive joy' (n. 1334).

The death and resurrection of Christ (or rather, Christ in his death and resurrection) are present for us to share. The active participation of all encouraged by the Second Vatican Council is not primarily about everyone having some special ministry to perform at every Mass, although the *Catechism* does teach that 'all have their own active parts to play in the celebration, each in his own way' (n. 1348). Full participation, however, is something much deeper.

The holy Eucharist completes Christian initiation. Those who have been raised to the dignity of the royal priesthood by Baptism, and configured more deeply to Christ by Confirmation, participate with the whole

community in the Lord's own sacrifice by means of
the Eucharist (n. 1322).

The Church as the Body of Christ participates in the
offering of her Head (n. 1368). In this sense we can call
the Eucharist the sacrifice of the Church; united with
Christ himself, we come to the Eucharist to be offered,
whole and entire, to the Father. True Christian
discipleship is not primarily following after Christ, or
imitating him, but being 'in Christ', being immersed,
plunged or inserted into the saving person and work of
Christ himself. It is in the liturgy, above all at our
baptism (cf. Rom 6:1-11) and in the Eucharist, that this is
made possible.

The Eucharistic Prayers get to the heart of the
meaning of the Mass. We ask that Christ 'make us an
everlasting gift' to the Father, by uniting us to his own
gift of himself (Eucharistic Prayer 3). We become 'a
living sacrifice of praise' (Eucharistic Prayer 4), united
with Jesus himself in his own worship of the Father. The
special Eucharistic Prayers for Reconciliation and for
Children are particularly helpful. The first prayer for
Masses with Children gives a neat summary of why we
should come to Mass:

We do now what Jesus told us to do.
We remember his death and resurrection

and we offer you, Father, the bread that gives us life
and the cup that saves us.
Jesus brings us to you;
welcome us as you welcome him.

By uniting ourselves with Christ in the Eucharist, as
Christ's Body with Christ our Head, we are taken up
'through him, with him, in him' into the heart of the
Father: we go where Jesus goes (cf. Jn 14:3), and we ask
the Father to 'accept us together with your beloved Son'
(Children 3; cf. Reconciliation 2).

The Church's living memory

The *Catechism* makes interesting use of the idea of
memory. From the Last Supper to the early and medieval
Church, to the Council of Trent and to today, the
Eucharist has remained much the same (n. 1345), and the
memory of what Jesus did (above all his death and
resurrection) is passed on in a living way from then until
now. 'The Holy Spirit is the Church's living memory' (n.
1099); it is because the Spirit is present in the Eucharist
as the living memory of the Church that the Eucharist
can be a memorial in the full sense of the word. The
whole Eucharist is very much the work of the Holy
Spirit. In the Liturgy of the Word, the Spirit 'recalls' all
that God has done for us, awakening the memory of the
Church and inspiring thanksgiving and praise (n. 1103).

But the liturgy is more than this: because in each celebration there is an outpouring of the Holy Spirit, the saving events we recall are 'actualised', made powerfully present (n. 1104). Through the sacraments the Holy Spirit makes present the wonders of God: it is above all in the Eucharist that 'The Spirit makes present and communicates the Father's work, fulfilled by the beloved Son' (n. 1155).

New meaning, new value

Although far from adequate on its own as an understanding of God's transforming work in the Eucharist, the giving of new meaning and value is an important aspect of the Spirit's work in the celebration. At the Last Supper Jesus 'gave a new and definitive meaning to the blessing of the bread and the cup' (n. 1334), and 'gave the Jewish Passover its definitive meaning' (n. 1340). People come to Mass seeking meaning for their lives, and a sense of value and worth for themselves. The Eucharist gives new meaning, and value to God's creation and to the people: 'the lives of the faithful, their praise, sufferings, prayer and work, are united with those of Christ and with his total offering, and so acquire a new value' (n. 1368).

In Eucharistic Prayer 2, we ask the Father to make us worthy, but we also thank him 'for counting us worthy to stand in your presence and serve you'. In the early

Church, standing was the Christian way to pray. To be allowed to stand in God's presence was a sign that God looked on us as his own sons and daughters. Nothing can affirm our dignity and value more strongly than taking part in the Eucharist and hearing what God says to us about ourselves.

The presence of Christ

The risen Christ is truly present in his Church in many ways: in the Scriptures, in the Church's prayer and worship 'where two or three are gathered in my name' (Mt 18:20) and in the poor, the sick and the imprisoned (Mt 25:31–46), in the sacraments and in his ministers. But he is present most especially and in a unique way under the Eucharistic species, the consecrated bread and wine: here in the blessed sacrament, 'the whole Christ is truly, really, and substantially contained' (n. 1374).

We believe this simply because Jesus says of the bread and wine: 'This is my body', 'This is my blood' (Mk 14:22–24). The risen Christ continues to say these words today through the ministry of his priests. Jesus himself is our bread of life (Jn 6:48). Take time to reflect prayerfully on the following passages from the New Testament: 1 Cor 10:16–17; 11:17–34; Jn 6:22–69; Lk 24:13–35.

Traditional Catholic theology distinguishes carefully between the 'accidents' or appearances of a thing (what our senses can grasp) and its 'substance', its ultimate reality. Although the appearances of bread and wine remain after the consecration, the deepest reality (or 'substance') of Christ's body and blood become present by the conversion of the deepest reality (or 'substance') of the bread and wine, a change usually referred to as 'transubstantiation':

> by the consecration of the bread and wine there takes place a change of the whole substance of the bread into the substance of the body of Christ our Lord and of the whole substance of the wine into the substance of his blood (n. 1376).

This conversion of the bread and wine into the Body and Blood of Christ happens 'in a way surpassing understanding' (n. 1333). The *Catechism* highlights the role of the Holy Spirit as the one who 'makes present the mystery of Christ, supremely in the Eucharist' (n. 737). The Western Church's focus on Christ's words of institution or consecration ('This is my Body', 'This is my Blood') and the Eastern Church's focus on the invocation of the Holy Spirit (the epiclesis) are woven together in the *Catechism*'s repeated teaching that the bread and wine become Christ's body and blood 'by the words of institution and the invocation of the Spirit' (nn. 1333, 1353, 1357, 1375). By the power of the Spirit and the words of Christ, Christ himself is 'really and mysteriously made present' (n. 1357).

Through faith not the senses

The whole living Christ is present in this sacrament in a way that can be grasped only by faith, not by our senses (n. 1381). The Catholic Church insists on three points here: the whole Christ is really and truly present (it is not just a 'spiritual' presence), but it is a presence *'in the manner of a substance'* (something beyond the senses, 'metaphysical') and it is a *sacramental presence* (the presence of an invisible reality through a visible sign). These three points must be held together.

As the *Catechism* puts it, 'Under the consecrated species of bread and wine Christ himself, living and glorious, is present in a true, real and substantial manner: his Body and Blood, with his soul and divinity' (n. 1413). This substantial presence of the risen and glorified Lord is there for us 'under the consecrated species'. Those species of bread and wine (their 'accidents', appearances, form: in other words, what our senses can grasp) are the sacramental sign, the 'Blessed Sacrament', of Christ's presence; they are not themselves that presence, as obviously 'the appearances of bread and wine' cannot possibly actually be 'the substance of the risen Christ'. But when we receive the consecrated bread and wine, the only 'substance' (or profound reality) that we receive is that of Christ himself.

Pope Paul VI reminded us in his encyclical letter
Mysterium Fidei that as a result of God's transforming
work in the Eucharist, the species of bread and wine take
on a new meaning, 'for they are no longer common bread
and common drink, but rather the sign of something
sacred and the sign of spiritual food' (art. 46). They take
on this new significance because they now contain and
make present a new reality: 'For beneath these
appearances there is no longer what was there before, but
something quite different'; in other words, instead of the
'substance' of bread and wine, there is now the
'substance' of Christ, whole and entire.

Historical thought

Throughout history there have been two extreme and
opposing tendencies in Eucharistic thought. One view so
stresses the distinction between the visible sign (the form,
species or 'accidents' of bread or wine) and the invisible
reality it signifies (the very presence of Christ) that the
two are seen as separate, with no guarantee that when we
receive the sacramental sign we also receive the Body
and Blood of Christ. This view does not take seriously
enough the real presence of the whole Christ in the
Eucharist, and often talks of simply the power or the
spirit of Jesus being present in some way.

The other view (sometimes called 'ultra-realism') so
strongly emphasises the real presence of Christ that the

visible sign and the invisible 'substance' of Christ become identified, with the unacceptable implication that whatever we do to the consecrated bread and wine – breaking, chewing, dropping, spilling, digesting – we do to Christ himself. This view takes seriously enough neither the substantial (beyond the senses) nature of Christ's presence, nor the central idea of sacrament (the invisible through the visible).

Great Catholic thinkers such as St Augustine and St Thomas Aquinas strongly affirmed the real presence of Christ in the Eucharist, but in a way which highlighted the sacramental nature of that presence and which avoided any crudely materialistic understanding. Some extreme realists in St Thomas' day were shocked by his interpretation, and his teaching is still rather challenging and disturbing for some Catholics today, both those who undermine Christ's presence in the Eucharist and those who hold on to an 'ultra-realist' view. His language of 'substance' and 'accidents' is not easy for us to grasp, but it enables us to insist on the real presence of Jesus through a change in the deepest reality of bread and wine while avoiding any crude identification of that presence with what we handle with our senses. The idea of 'sacrament' is vital: it involves a distinction – but not a separation – between the visible sign (what we see, touch and taste) and the invisible reality we receive (the whole Christ). This saves us from the pitfall of thinking that whatever is done to what we handle is actually being done to the risen Lord himself. The *Catechism* reminds us that the whole Christ is present in the Eucharistic elements, but 'in such a way that the breaking of the bread does not divide Christ' (n. 1377).

Reception and Adoration

We are urged to receive communion each time we come to Mass (n. 1388). Christ is sacramentally present both under the form of bread and under the form of wine, and therefore we receive 'all the fruit of Eucharistic grace' by communion under the form of bread alone. The *Catechism* reminds us, however, that 'the sign of communion is more complete when given under both kinds, since in that form the sign of the Eucharistic meal appears more clearly' (n. 1390).

Whatever way we receive communion, it is Christ himself that we receive, and it is important that we prepare ourselves for so holy a moment. The one hour's fast before receiving communion – hardly a great inconvenience – helps us to think about the meaning of what we are to do. Simple things like: what we wear, how we participate, are meant to express 'the respect, solemnity and joy' of the Eucharist. What matters most, however, is our inward preparation, allowing our hearts, minds and lives to be purified, renewed and opened to the presence of Christ.

Catholics express their faith in the Eucharistic presence of Christ by signs of adoration such as genuflecting or bowing deeply. This special presence of Christ begins at the consecration and lasts as long as the Eucharistic elements (n. 1377). This is why Catholics worship the Lord present under the sacramental signs, not only during the Mass itself but also afterwards. Christ gives us his sacramental presence as one of the ways in which he is with us, even to the end of time (Mt 28.20); he waits for us in this sacrament of love, inviting us to meet him in adoration:

> In his Eucharistic presence he remains mysteriously in our midst as the one who loved us and gave himself up for us, and he remains under signs that express and communicate this love (n. 1380).

Christ the Priest

The Eucharist is the heart of the life of the priest, and it is in presiding at the Eucharist that the special ministry of priests is most evident (n. 1142). At the Eucharist the priest does not replace an absent Christ; he is the sacramental sign and instrument of the presence of Christ as our Head and Shepherd:

> At its head is Christ himself, the principle agent of the Eucharist. He is high priest of the New Covenant; it is

he himself who presides invisibly over every
Eucharistic celebration (n. 1348).

This is important. When we come to Mass, the One who
invites us, gathers us together, presides over us, teaches,
nourishes and blesses us, is Christ himself. He does this in
a special way through the visible priest, and it is obviously
the ideal that the priest himself should be a good sign and
instrument of Christ – a friendly and welcoming person, a
good preacher, a true shepherd who knows and cares for
his flock. No priest is perfect; every priest is a sinner and
has his faults and weaknesses. If your priest does not
match up to the ideal, and the celebration of the Mass is
not as you might like, that is no good reason not to take
part in that Mass. The risen Lord himself is there inviting
us to be part of his community, to play our part in the
celebration, to listen to his Word, to share in his saving
sacrifice, to receive his gift of himself, to be sent forth into
the world in his name. The sacrament of ordination
guarantees that when a priest presides at the Eucharist,
Christ invisibly presides through him. Everything we say
about the Eucharist is possible only because Christ himself
is there among us, powerfully at work.

The Mass of all Ages

The history of the Mass is a fascinating subject, and one
we cannot pursue here. There have been all kinds of

changes down through the centuries, not just in our own time, but the substance of the Eucharist has not changed (nn. 1345–7, 1356). The Eucharist of the first Christians, the Eucharist described by St Justin and St Hippolytus in the second and third centuries, the Eucharist of the Middle Ages and that laid down after the Council of Trent, the Eucharist as renewed by Pope Paul VI after the Second Vatican Council and celebrated today; each is the same Mass of all Ages, the same Eucharist of Jesus Christ.'

The *Catechism* points out that the Eucharist today has the same basic movement as the Easter meal which the risen Jesus ate with his disciples after his encounter with them on the road to Emmaus (Lk 24:13–35):

> Walking with them he explained the Scriptures to them; sitting with them at table 'he took bread, blessed and broke it, and gave it to them' (n. 1347).

Communion with Christ

We receive Holy Communion above all in order to grow closer to Jesus Christ (n. 1391), sharing his life and deepening our friendship with him (n. 1395).

The celebration of the Eucharistic sacrifice is wholly directed toward the intimate union of the faithful with Christ himself through communion. To receive communion is to receive Christ himself who has offered himself for us (n. 1382).

Sometimes people stop going to Mass because they say that they 'get nothing out of it'. This often means that they have not come away with their hearts uplifted, with great feelings of spiritual nourishment. They blame boring celebrations, tedious preaching, uninspiring music, lack of a sense of community, hypocrisy, unsympathetic priests. These are sometimes valid criticisms, and priests and people have a responsibility to put all of their gifts and talents into the greatest thing they do together – celebrating the Eucharist. But flaws and failings in our way of celebrating the Mass are no good reason for opting out. The Eucharist is as vital to our spiritual life as ordinary food is to our physical and mental life: 'What material food produces in our bodily life, Holy Communion wonderfully achieves in our spiritual life' (n. 1392). We would be foolish to give up eating and drinking simply because most meals were uninspiring.

Christ offers us himself in the Eucharist, and that regular feeding on Christ is as vital to our spiritual journey as the daily diet of manna (far from inspiring fodder, however much it came 'from heaven') was to the forty-year desert journey of God's chosen people. Christ is our life, and without him we die.

The Last Supper was the last of many meals that Jesus ate with his friends. They were accustomed to being with him at table, listening to him, breaking bread with him, sharing their lives with him. Once they knew that he was risen from the dead, alive with them in a new way, it was natural that they should want to continue these intimate meals with their Lord. When we come to Mass, to the Lord's Supper, we join the apostles, the saints throughout the ages, and the Church throughout the world to be together with our Risen Lord, to listen to his Word, to share his life given for us and to open our lives to his presence.

Communion with one another

The Eucharist also leads to unity with one another in Christ, the unity of the Body of Christ:

> Those who receive the Eucharist are united more closely to Christ. Through it Christ unites them to all the faithful in one body – the Church. Communion renews, strengthens and deepens this incorporation into the Church, already achieved by Baptism (n. 1396).

Communion with Christ in his sacrifice and communion with one another go hand in hand, as St Paul clearly taught:

> The cup of blessing that we bless, is it not a sharing in the blood of Christ? The bread that we break, is it not a sharing in the body of Christ? Because there is one bread, we who are many are one body, for we all partake of the one bread (1 Cor 10:16–17).

Eucharistic Prayer 2 asks that 'all of us who share in the body and blood of Christ be brought together in unity by the Holy Spirit', and that we may grow together in love. By receiving together the body of Christ, we become together the body of Christ, the Church.

Do we see deepening communion between the members of our Eucharistic communities as a central purpose of the Eucharist? How does that affect the way we celebrate? The Catholic Church understands the Eucharist as 'properly the sacrament of those who are in full communion with the Church' (n. 1395), and this is the main reason why we cannot normally share Eucharistic communion with other Christians. But how much effort do we as Catholics put into being in full communion with each other – full communion of faith and love even in our own parish community?

It is at the Eucharist that we are most truly Christ's Body. The Eucharist is the supreme expression of the nature and mission of the Church. It is at Mass that we see what the Church is all about, and everything else we do as Christ's Church flows from and leads back to the celebration of Mass. What does the way your particular parish celebrates the Eucharist reveal about the kind of Christian community you are?

The *Catechism* sees the pain of division between Christians, experienced with particular intensity when we cannot share Eucharistic communion together, as spurring us on to more urgent prayer for complete unity (n. 1398). There are established norms for 'Eucharistic hospitality' with other Christians under special circumstances. This is easier with the Eastern Orthodox Churches whose ordained ministry and celebration of the Eucharist are accepted as valid by the Catholic Church, but there are also particular occasions when other Christians who have a catholic faith in the Eucharist may receive communion from a Catholic minister (n. 1399f; cf. *Code of Canon Law*, 844.4; *Directory for the Application of Principles and Norms on Ecumenism*, 122–136, 159–160).

Communion with the poor and oppressed

The *Catechism* situates the Eucharist firmly in the real world. The Eucharist commits us to the poor: 'To receive in truth the Body and Blood of Christ given up for us, we must recognise Christ in the poorest, his brethren' (n. 1397). It is not enough to recognise the real presence of Christ in the 'breaking of bread', to reverence him in the Blessed Sacrament; we are only truly Eucharistic people if our reception of Christ leads us to recognise and reverence his presence in the broken lives of those around us, and to seek real communion with those in need. We are called to balance our prayerful adoration of Christ in the Blessed Sacrament with our loving service of Christ in those with whom he personally identifies: 'Whatever you do for the least of my brothers and sisters, you do to me… Whatever you fail to do for the least of my brothers and sisters, you fail to do to me' (Mt 25:40, 45). Any parish which has true adoration of Christ in the Blessed Sacrament will be a parish actively dedicated to loving service of the poor and oppressed at home and overseas - the homeless and rejected, the sick and the sad. The deeply Eucharistic person will be the one, for example, who reaches out in welcome to the person with AIDS, seeking - with Christ - not to condemn but to share that person's life.

In the Eucharist, we are united with the suffering of Christ, not only on his cross but in those people being 'crucified' today. If the Eucharist is the living memorial of Christ's Cross, we must stand at the foot of the cross of the poor and oppressed, sharing their suffering and acting in love for their deliverance: 'In the Eucharist, the Church is, as it were, at the foot of the cross with Mary, united with the offering and intercession of Christ' (n. 1370).

'Ite, missa est'

The Eucharist is called the Mass (*Missa*) because it 'concludes with the sending forth (*missio*) of the faithful into the world, so that they may fulfil God's will in their daily lives' (n. 1332). We leave the celebration as people sent by Christ to bring him to others, and in a sense to be him for others. We receive the sacramental presence of Christ in the Eucharist in order to be together the sacramental presence of Christ in the world. At the end of each Mass, Jesus says to us, 'As the Father sent me, so am I sending you' (Jn 20:21; cf. 17:18). The celebration of Mass may be ended, but we 'go in peace to love and to serve the Lord'.

A service to others

We do not come to Mass purely for our own spiritual benefit, or even for that of our particular parish community. We celebrate the Eucharist for the salvation of the human race, for both the living and the dead, and making the effort to take part in the Mass is a service to others. Through our simple celebrations of the Eucharist, the saving power of Christ's sacrifice radiates out to 'advance the peace and salvation of all the world' (Eucharistic Prayer 3).

Coming to Mass is also one of the most important ways in which we bear witness to Christ before the world. Simply by being there together at the Eucharist, professing and celebrating our faith, we stand up for what we believe. In past centuries, Catholics have been put to death because they insisted on risking everything to take part in the Mass in times of persecution. For young people who have just been confirmed, for others who simply do not have the time or health to be actively involved in all kinds of Church activities and ministries, and indeed for every Catholic, the most public way to witness to our faith is to celebrate the Eucharist together, especially on Sundays. There are some, even friends and family, who will think it strange, even laughable, and for many young people today the decision to come to Mass demands a courage not unlike that of the martyrs. But there is no greater sign of life in a parish than to see young people at Mass together.

Forward to the Future

The Eucharist is also a pledge of the glory to come, 'an anticipation of the heavenly glory' (n. 1402) which anticipates the future wedding feast of the Lamb (n. 1329). This dimension of the Eucharist is important, and needs further reflection by each of us:

> Thus from celebration to celebration, as they proclaim the Paschal mystery of Jesus until he comes, the pilgrim people of God advances, following the narrow way of the cross, towards the heavenly banquet, when all the elect will be seated at the table of the kingdom (n. 1344).

If the Eucharist today is both a memorial of Easter and an anticipation of the final Wedding Feast of heaven, then joy (in its deepest sense) should be a characteristic of every celebration (cf. n. 1616). It may not always seem so, but when we come to Mass 'we already unite ourselves with the heavenly liturgy and anticipate eternal life, when God will be all in all' (n. 1326). The ancient prayer *O Sacrum Convivium* is a good summary of the past, present and future dimensions of the Eucharist:

> At this sacred banquet in which Christ is received,
> the memory of his passion is renewed,
> our lives are filled with grace,
> and a promise of future glory is given to us.

Sacrament of Love

One key and recurring theme in the *Catechism*'s treatment of the Eucharist is love. This illustrates its fundamentally positive approach to the Eucharist and to the whole of our faith. Christ has given us the Eucharist as a 'pledge of his love' (n. 1337):

> [He] wanted us to have the memorial of the love with which he loved us to the end. In his Eucharistic presence he remains mysteriously in our midst as the one who loved us and gave himself up for us, and he remains under signs that express and communicate this love (n. 1380).

The Eucharist is the 'sacrament of love' which revives our own love (n. 1394) and which teaches us that all real love always involves listening, openness, sacrificial self-giving and sharing one's life with another.

The Prologue to the *Catechism* ends with these words from the Roman Catechism of 1566:

The whole concern of doctrine and its teaching must be directed to the love that never ends. Whether something is proposed for belief, for hope or for action, the love of our Lord must always be made accessible, so that anyone can see that all the works of perfect Christian virtue spring from love and have no other objective than to arrive at love (n. 25).

This applies in a special way to the Church's teaching on the Eucharist. Once we understand the Eucharist in this way, it will be obvious why the Catholic Church emphasises so strongly that regular participation in the Eucharist is vital for maintaining and deepening our life together in Christ. It is there above all that the Risen Christ is present for us, drawing us ever deeper into the mystery of his saving love, ever deeper into the life of the Living God: 'The Church knows that the Lord comes even now in the Eucharist, and that he is there in our midst' (n. 1404).